Starry Jones Kicks Cancer's Butt

Starry Jones Kicks Cancer's Butt

Linda Eckert Sawka

Starry Jones Kicks Cancer's Butt

ISBN -13: 978-1517315566

ISBN -10: 1517315565

Printed in the United States of America

Whenever there is a problem.....

Repeat over and over:

All is well.

Everything is working out for my highest good.

Out of this situation only good will come.

I am safe!

It will work miracles in your life.

Louise L. Hay

TABLE OF CONTENTS

FOREWORD

In the course of miracles seen over forty years of practice, there are always patients who develop a special relationship and bond with their doctor to become friends. As a Doctor of Chiropractic Medicine, I have been extremely blessed to be overflowing with patients who have touched me as deeply as I have touched them. Linda Sawka is one of these extraordinary beings who make living so worthwhile.

We met in June 2009 in Antigua when she came to the day spa for chiropractic care. I fly to Antigua once a month from Dominica for a week of seeing patients. Linda was very familiar with chiropractic care as she had been adjusted in the past and her nursing background afforded her easy conversation in technical terms that delighted both of us. Linda was very accepting of the wholistic approach I presented including diet and nutrition, exercise and fitness, stress management, Reiki, muscle testing, among many others. As the rigors of her profession and traveling at times caused her more stress, I was able to suggest self-help techniques for her to use on a regular basis.

After two years of seeing her once a month, Linda announced that her tumor markers had jumped which indicated a strong likelihood of recurrence of her granulosa cell tumor.

She was emotionally concerned at the serious ramifications of this as was I. Some of our discussions were very deep about life's purpose, dying, and loving. We realized that when you have an "*in*curable disease" you must go "*in*side" to cure it and work in some "*in*visible realms". We had long talks about how she felt in her body, to trust her intuitive wisdom and to put the lab tests in context so as not to put all her trust in them only.

There were other times when the tumor markers went up and down, but Linda had committed to live her life in the moment with as much joy, beauty, and laughter as she could create on a daily basis. As Linda's attitude improved dramatically, she found an online course to become an Integrative Nutrition Health and Wellness coach. I was extremely happy and supportive of her decision. I watched with infinite gratitude as this wonderful woman blossomed into a health advocate, NOT fighting against cancer, but living fully in the moment. She even began to come into her appointments with no misalignment as her body worked at maximum efficiency. It has been a spiritual transformation!

In her most current lab tests, the tumors have stopped growing, while Linda has begun even more growing by taking time to write a book of her incredible journey into the light of love and healing. I applaud her dedication, joyfulness and above all I am honored to write this forward of her book.

What I know for sure is that all speed bumps on the journey and adventure called LIFE are by "Divine Design". Throughout our ongoing relationship, it became very clear that it "takes a village" to heal a soul. Many people have played a part in this story and that is what makes it so rich and Linda so blessed.

Dr. Janet S. Taylor

Wholistic Doctor of Chiropractic

Roseau, Commonwealth of Dominica

www.quantumleap@cwdom.dm

Introduction

I was about four or five years old when I had a look alike by the name of Starry Jones. Since no one could tell us apart, we would switch out with each other. My mother never knew which one of us she was dealing with until she called me to some task and I would respond that "I'm not Linda, she's gone away for a while. I'm Starry Jones!" And then Starry Jones would complete the requested task but with a flourish! She was extremely helpful and courteous – the best little assistant anyone could have. I believe Starry Jones must have been a movie star. She loved dressing in long, flowing skirts with jewelry and a shawl. Starry Jones loved life and lived it to the fullest (as her stories would tell) – she had no fears – she could do anything. She was here one minute and gone the next - you never knew when she might suddenly be called away to a new adventure and Linda would return.

In the spring of my 6th year, my father, an officer in the US Air Force, was re-assigned from the Pentagon to Naples, Italy. Our family boarded a Navy ship bound for Europe and Starry Jones was never heard from again.

Recently, some sixty years later, there has been some glimmerings, some bubbling up from the spirit of that same Starry Jones.

Why has it taken so long for Starry to reappear? What happened in the first place that made her disappear? I guess life just gets in the way – life and the responsibilities that go along with it, blocking out that unique, authentic 'self' that we were all born with, the one that sees life with child-like wonder, curiosity and joy.

This is my story – Linda's story – a story of life's ups and downs that come and go until one day, one particular challenge momentarily stops you in your tracks – as if you unknowingly walked into a glass door – the day you learn you have cancer.

Surprisingly, this isn't a sad story, although there surely were sad moments. This is a story of Great Learning – of challenges and changes.

Let me please say here that I can offer no promise of cures, as each of us are on our own unique journey on this earthly plain, one designed specifically for us – one that we can either fight "tooth and nail" to our dying day or one that we can embrace, deciding to become the hero or heroine rather than the victim. What I do hope to offer is a path to freedom – freedom from helplessness, hopelessness, powerlessness, a lessening of fear, a path to being the best that you can be, a body, mind and soul that is ripe for miracles.

So....let's get started, shall we?

Chapter 1

MY STORY

In the beginning I believe that most of us are born healthy and whole – especially if our mothers were careful to nourish themselves and their yet-to-be-born child.

In my case, I was a healthy seven pounder, nourished from the breast and yet, like all my female siblings, had pretty severe infantile eczema, a red, itchy rash of the skin. For some reason, the youngest, my brother, escaped from this annoyance.

We had the normal childhood illnesses of the day – measles, mumps, chicken pox – and got all the vaccines when they became available.

Being one of five children, there wasn't an excessive amount of individual attention – unless, of course, you were ill; then you were cuddled and loved and read to, served special meals on a tray in your bed. You were truly made to feel special. It wasn't till more than half a century later that a thunderbolt hit me. It was when I was sick that I most felt loved – Wow! (Do you see where I'm going with this?) This went so far as to mean that even in our childhood make-believe play, I would frequently be the one with some pitiable disease – Yikes!

After graduating from high school, I somewhat skeptically, chose nursing as a career. Barely a month into my studies and I knew this was the field I was destined for – I loved caring for people and doing my best to ease their fear and pain. Most of my working life was spent in high stress areas like Intensive and Cardiac Care and I thought I thrived on it.

Despite loving my career, I couldn't wait to be married and start a family and finally, in my late twenties, thought I'd found my ideal mate. After six months of bliss, the troubles began and two years and much heartache later, I was divorced.

In my thirties, I met a gentle, kindred soul and married again. A few years later, we moved away from the hustle and bustle of the Washington, D.C. area to the quiet island of Antigua. We were members of the Baha'i Faith and wanted to live and serve mankind in an underdeveloped country. Ours became a much simpler life, blessed by so much physical beauty. Still as many of us do, we had a hard time deciding where to draw the line in our work and service, not even knowing the meaning of self-care. There were many years of financial struggle, never quite being able to make ends meet.

When our children spread their wings and left the nest, there were new challenges – my husband and I looked at each other and realized, apart from the children and our Faith, we had nothing in common.

We had nothing to talk about that would interest each other. Rather than facing this problem, we each turned to our work and formed our own outside friendships, spending little time together nourishing our own.

It was a series of health crises that initially brought about the first steps in repairing our marriage. During this period of discontent, I might call it, I had several episodes of sudden, severe, low abdominal pain. After a few minutes, it would spread over the entire abdominal area and I would feel like I had swallowed a sharp knitting needle! Usually within twenty minutes, the pain would start to subside and after a few hours, I was back to normal. The second time this happened, I decided to see my gynecologist and she confirmed by ultrasound that I had apparently ruptured an ovarian cyst. I believe it was at that time that she put me on Hormone Replacement Therapy (HRT) for a while but then I decided there was too much adverse publicity about HRT – I'd rather do without.

In 2001, there was a particularly severe episode of another ruptured ovarian cyst and this time further investigation led to the discovery of an abdominal mass – that dreaded word! Surgery was quickly scheduled and, as I was past childbearing age, it was felt that the best plan was to do a complete hysterectomy and oophorectomy (removal of uterus and ovaries). In my first post-operative visit with the physician to get the sutures out, she read me the preliminary histology report.

In her matter-of-fact manner, she related that the report was indecisive – whether the mass was from Small Cell Cancer or Granulosa Cell Tumor (GCT). I sat there in shock, barely hearing her, when she told me the samples were being sent on to Cambridge, England, for a final determination. I had NO idea there was even a possibility of cancer! Next came a nerve-wracking ten day period of intense prayers while we awaited a second opinion. When the verdict came in, we all breathed a huge sigh of relief – it was NOT Small Cell Cancer, it was GCT. And I thought that was the end of that!

Six months later, my doctor called me. She had just been informed by the pathologist that this type of tumor can recur, but that there was a blood test that worked for most women, as a tumor marker. She recommended getting this blood test every six months. It was very expensive, as it had to be sent away, but when I could afford it, I got it done.

A few years later, a routine blood test on my husband brought us back to crisis mode when we discovered his platelet count was dangerously low. Several tests later, we learned the heartbreaking news that he had Hepatitis C and was in End Stage Liver Disease – there was nothing that could be done for him unless he qualified for a liver transplant! How could someone get to this point without our even having any suspicions? And me a nurse, for God's sake!!??

The next year was a roller coaster ride that had us thoroughly wrung out emotionally. First came the rush move back to the US to see what medical help we could find for my husband. The good news was that he qualified for VA care being a Vietnam era veteran. The bad news was that it took about six months of testing before we even knew if he qualified for a liver transplant. That meant we now had to set up housekeeping in Florida and I had to get a job, to support us during this time. After months of testing, we learned that he did qualify for a liver transplant but that the waiting list was five years long and that his lab values were such that he was actually too good to put on the waiting list! This news made our spirits plummet as we would have to sit here, in the US, on somebody's back burner, until my husband's condition deteriorated so much that he would actually qualify to be listed on a list that was already five years long! That was what we were told one day, and the very next we were told that the latest ultrasound revealed a spot that was likely to be liver cancer. We were devastated to say the least but then the doctors told us that if a biopsy confirmed that diagnosis, it would bump him to the top of the transplant list! Talk about an emotional roller coaster!

A few weeks later, my husband underwent a surgery to "ablate" the liver cancer tumor and a mere three weeks later, before he had totally recovered from that surgery, we got *THE* call. The call we both prayed for and feared.

There was a liver….a young fellow a few hours away had been involved in a serious motor vehicle accident – there was no hope of recovery. His grieving parents made the difficult decision to donate his organs. The liver was a match!

Fast forward over the next year and a half – a period of frequent trips to Richmond, where the transplant was done and follow-up was conducted, a time of juggling my job as care giver to a newly transplanted patient and my other job as a full-time nurse in a VA hospital. It certainly left no time for remembering that I was supposed to be getting those blood tests and besides, I was months away from the 5 year mark – wasn't that supposed to mean you were home free?

When I finally remembered to get the test, we were about to travel home to Antigua for our first visit post-transplant. My doctor in the US pronounced my test results normal but as a courtesy, I shared them with my Antigua doctor. She phoned me up, quite upset – saying the results were significantly elevated and I needed to get a CT scan as soon as possible, to look for tumors.

As soon as I returned to the US, I was linked up with a gynecological oncologist (Wait! Aren't those the doctors who deal with cancer??). She explained that these tumors can come back, sometimes staying in the abdomen and sometimes spreading to the lungs and/or liver, at which point they become inoperable.

My CT scans revealed a grapefruit-sized tumor in the abdomen, with several smaller ones in the same area. She went on to explain that chemo was sometimes used but wasn't very effective, nor was radiation. The best plan was vigilance by those tumor marker blood tests, followed by CT scans when the results were elevated and then surgery whenever a tumor was spotted. A week later, I had my second surgery for this disease – this time necessitating the removal of a portion of my colon. But I was tremendously relieved that the doctor was able to piece together the colon and I didn't end up with a colostomy. The histology once again confirmed that it was the same granulosa cell tumors.

This wonderful doctor put the fear of God in me that the tumors could come back and that I must religiously get my blood tests done every three months now.

Barely a year later, following two emergent hospitalizations for my husband, who was now undergoing the Ribavirin/ Interferon treatment (as the Hepatitis C had come back and was even more aggressively attacking the new liver), my tumor markers jumped up. My doctor was calling for more CT scans, and although I was 'freaked' that my disease was coming back so soon, some little internal voice was telling me there had to be some kind of correlation here – between our recent increase in stressors and my markers becoming elevated. Coincidentally (is there really such a thing?), I came across an article about belly fat and the fact that it releases hormones.

I looked up information on what my tumor markers tracked – my type of tumor releases estrogen...so does belly fat! And now, reflecting back on my husband's hospitalizations - he had no appetite. I knew he needed nourishment and the hospital food was not providing it. In fact, one meal I'll never forget...they brought him a hotdog on a hard, stale bun, tater tots and a chocolate éclair! So, every day I brought him food I knew he'd love...hamburgers with all the trimmings from his favorite "Checkers Fast Food"...but I didn't stop there – I got the curly fries and milk shake too! And...I couldn't let him eat it alone...so I got the same for myself. The next day it might be a Haagen-Dazs bar...and of course, one for myself too! It went on like that for a few more days and miraculously my husband got well! (Not from the hamburgers and fries, I might add, but because they found the strange little virus that was making him so sick and finally put him on the right antibiotic to deal with it.) Is it any wonder that my markers went up? I gained ten pounds! Ten pounds of hormone-excreting belly fat!

About that time, a dear friend was looking like she was losing weight, appearing younger, happier and healthier every time I met up with her. I asked her for her secret and that's what led me to making the first step in taking charge of my own health!

CHAPTER 2

TAKING CHARGE

MaryJane's secret was a book called *Eat to Live* by Dr. Joel Fuhrman. She said you have to give up meat, dairy and sugar. I said, "No Way!" Never in my life have I been the least bit interested in becoming a vegetarian. And what about yogurt? Isn't that what all those centenarians in Russia ate? And don't even get me started on sugar! I come from a long line of sweet tooth fanatics and chocoholics. I used to supplement my income by making desserts for restaurants and cakes for special occasions! And what self-respecting dessert chef would possibly be able to say "No, thank you" to sampling some little sugary delight?

But then again, the thought of the tumor returning and possibly facing another surgery so soon after the last one was definitely worth some drastic action. I called my doctor and offered a plea bargain – give me six weeks and then let's repeat the blood test. If the numbers are up, I'll go ahead with the CT scan, but maybe, just maybe, the numbers will be down and I will have found the cure for my disease.

Once the decision was made, I couldn't wait to get started. I drove right over to the nearest Barnes & Noble, found the book, made my purchase and then sat out in the parking lot, speed reading for the next hour.

I was trying to fast forward to what I *could and should* be eating so that I could go to the grocery store.

Finally, on p. 197, I found the "Weekly Shopping List:"

- Canned beans – I bought chick peas, black beans and red beans

- Frozen vegetables – don't think I bought many of those other than some spinach and peas

- Lots of low sugar fruits – strawberries, grapefruit, melons and blueberries

- Fresh vegetables to be eaten raw – carrots, celery, peppers, tomatoes, mushrooms, snow peas, Romaine lettuce and lots of it!

- Fresh vegetables to cook – eggplant, cabbage, broccoli, string beans, zucchini, spinach, onions, acorn squash, garlic (I had not heard of kale yet so didn't buy any of that or some of the other wonderful greens I now love)

- Whole wheat pita bread

- Sesame seeds, sunflower seeds, walnuts and ground flaxseed

- Oatmeal

- Tofu or TVP (total vegetable protein) I felt too inexperienced to try that just yet

There were other things on Dr. Fuhrman's list but either they were things I didn't like – like canned Chinese vegetables and frozen broccoli - or there were things I had never tried like shiitake mushrooms, turnips and tofu.

Now that I had my food, I had to come up with a meal plan. My family had already made it abundantly clear that I'd be going down this meatless road on my own – so it would mean two meal preparations each night. I thumbed through the book some more and got to the Do's and Don'ts:

Actually it was more like foods that were unlimited:

- All raw vegetables – goal 1 lb. a day!

- Cooked green vegetables – goal 1 lb. a day!

- Beans, legumes, bean sprouts and tofu – 1 cup daily

- Fresh fruit – at least 4 servings a day

And foods that were limited:

- Cooked starchy vegetables or whole grains – no more than one serving a day (butternut or acorn squash, corn, potatoes, breads, cereals)

- Raw nuts and seeds – 1 ounce maximum per day

- Avocado – 2 ounces maximum a day

- Ground flaxseed – 1 tablespoon per day

And foods that were OFF LIMITS:

- Dairy products

- Animal products

- Between meal snacks

- Fruit juice or dried fruit

Dr. Fuhrman's Ten Tips for Living with the Six Week Plan were most helpful:

1. Remember the salad is the main dish – eat it first at lunch and dinner

2. Eat as much fruit as you want but at least 4 fresh fruits daily

3. Variety is the spice of life, particularly when it comes to greens

4. Beware of the starchy vegetable

5. Eat beans or legumes every day – at least 1 cup

6. Eliminate animal and dairy (there it is again!)

7. Have a tablespoon of ground flaxseed every day – I put it on my oats

8. Consume nuts and seeds in limited amounts, no more than 1 ounce daily. I put walnuts on my oats and sunflower seeds in my salads

9. Eat lots of mushrooms all the time

10. Keep it simple!

The first night was probably the hardest – eating my big salad, half a cup of rice with half a cup of beans, cooked vegetable and watching the rest of the family with their pork chops, potatoes, etc. However, when it came time for dessert, everyone enjoyed my big, colorful, fruit salad.

Day 2 was a Monday so I got up earlier than usual, made my delicious breakfast of ½ grapefruit and oatmeal with walnuts, raisins (okay – I guess I cheated here on the "no dried fruits"), ground flax seed and a touch of honey. Then I made my lunch to take to work. I filled a good-sized bowl with cut up Romaine lettuce, (washed and bagged the night before), added tomatoes, cucumbers, celery, mushrooms, radishes and topped it off with the other half of the pink grapefruit cut into small pieces. I found with the juicy grapefruit bits I didn't need any salad dressing but these days, one would probably be encouraged to add some extra virgin olive oil. I took the half cup of beans in a small container to add at lunchtime.

The last item was the half slice of the whole grain pita and I was ready for my first lunch day adventure. Would I be full? – Would I get hungry in an hour? – Could I make it to dinner time?

Lunch time came and my co-workers were quick to notice that instead of trekking down to the cafeteria, I was eating at my desk. Raised eyebrows and doubtful looks were my lunch time companions. After lunch, I experienced something new – I was ENERGIZED! I felt full enough but without that heavy, "I need a nap" feeling. While my co-workers dragged through the afternoon, frequently hitting up the coffee pot, I cheerfully breezed through the rest of my day. Amazing! I didn't get hungry!

A big surprise greeted me at home that evening – my husband decided to join me in my new culinary adventure and by the week's end, my daughter decided to join us too! The only holdout was our four year old grandson, the carnivore! That kid could put away a half pound of bacon on a Sunday morning and be asking for more! So for him, an occasional piece of meat made it to the table – on the other nights, we had to put up with the big pout!

Once I'd settled into my new dietary routine, I thought it might be time to actually read Dr. Fuhrman's book! Mostly, it was a page turner and an eye opener. He was absolutely right that, before the end of the first week, I no longer had any cravings – whether it was for meat, sweets or even chocolate! Shocking!

Six weeks went by quite effortlessly. The only real challenges were the dinner meals – we were so accustomed to eating only one vegetable per meal that I frequently had to remind my husband (the chief cook and bottle washer) that we were supposed to be eating more vegetables, and to at least double up!

People noticed. We all were getting compliments on how well we looked, the pounds we lost, our clear complexions, such energy. But what really sold us on our newfound vegetarianism was when six weeks later, my tumor marker results came in – they were back down to baseline! Yippee!! I thought I'd possibly found the cure to my disease! The only change I made to my dietary regimen after the six weeks were over was in the form of a small Dove dark chocolate heart – one after lunch and one after dinner – just for heart health, you know!

By this time in my nursing career, I was a Research Nurse. I was convinced that eating this way was the cure to a whole list of diseases – hypertension, diabetes, obesity, to name a few. I would have loved to start my own research project within the VA – a project that would house interested veterans away from their normal surrounds for several weeks. Initially, all their food would be prepared for them and every day there would be classes on why's and how to's of eating such a nutrient dense diet. By the second week you would have them preparing their own meals.

Maybe for those interested, you could have them stay a third week to start out a new group of veterans – to assist with the meal preparation and classes. The subjects would be followed over a period of time, evaluating their blood work, blood pressure, weight, well-being and any other symptoms. Hopefully, they would have been armed with enough knowledge and the desire to continue, to be able to steer clear of the local McDonalds or Burger King! Funnily enough, there was no interest in a research project that wasn't connected with a big drug company with the money to fund it.

My doctor was pleased that my markers had come down and always smiled at my enthusiastic desire and determination to find a cure for my disease but I believe it was her nurse practitioner who said to me that my dietary changes would certainly do no harm but ultimately there is no cure for this disease. Although I intended to prove her wrong, that little seed of doubt had been planted and every once in a while would pop up.

Six months into our new way of eating came another huge confirmation; on Thanksgiving Day. (Yes! We broke down and had turkey – some traditions must absolutely be maintained!) So, on Thanksgiving Day my husband's doctor, the liver specialist, called. Being Peruvian, he didn't realize the sacrilege of working on this special day. He had just been reviewing my husband's latest lab results and was calling to tell us that Charlie was CURED!

Cured from Hepatitis C, a disease we were told was incurable?? Whoever heard of such a thing? The doctor, of course, attributed it to the Interferon/ Ribavirin treatment that had been stopped five months earlier when my husband got so sick. However, in our jubilant celebration that Thanksgiving Day, we felt that a significant role had been played by our new, liver supportive, way of eating.

As I reflect back on that time, there had been another affirmation of this way of eating. Two years earlier, I had been diagnosed with osteoporosis after a bone density scan. I was put on that treatment Sally Fields was pushing, I think it was Boniva, but after several months the muscle, joint and bone aches were too much to bear. I decided I'd rather take my chances with osteoporosis! When I had my next bone density test two years later, it showed complete reversal of the disease – no more osteoporosis! That's the power of raw broccoli for you!

With all this good news, we felt it was finally time to pack up and return to our beloved Antigua.

Chapter 3

THE RETURN – in more ways than one!

The triumphant return was just in time for Christmas. What a wonderful time to celebrate all our victories – Charlie's successful liver transplant and ultimate cure from Hepatitis C, and for me, the reversal of my osteoporosis and hopeful cure from my GCT disease. We were happy to share our new way of eating with anyone who enquired. We knew it might be a bit of a challenge – finding adequate amounts of fresh, local vegetables, especially lettuce, but we brought lots of seed packets home with us and had all the good intentions of becoming backyard farmers.

We soon learned that we did not leave all stressors behind. First there was the exorbitant duty that was charged on all our used belongings that we brought home with us; next we needed to buy at least one car, more likely two. I was thrilled to get my old job back but quickly learned that the money didn't nearly go as far now that the government had instituted many new taxes – including one on groceries! Our savings were, little by little, being wiped out.

Three months into our new "old life," we came to the realization that we could not sustain ourselves on my meager salary, so I reluctantly took a job that was at once our greatest blessing but also a source of some really big stressors – physical, mental and emotional.

I worked very hard as the only medical person on a US Air Force Base, responsible for about 145 fellow employees. On the good side was all the wonderful benefits that came with this job – a one-time duty free concession on a car (that solved one of our problems!), three free trips to Florida per year, health and life insurance, and a Florida mailing address that enabled Amazon.com to become my new best friend. On the down side, were the long hours, the being on-call 24 hours a day, seven days a week and the stress that came with a new climate of super accountability within the Air Force which manifested as frequent, unexpected inspections and the demand for even more paperwork documentation.

Another mixed blessing of this job was that meals were provided. Although much of the food was good, it certainly would not have been approved by Dr. Fuhrman! When I first started, I don't recall ever seeing anything but iceberg lettuce – there are very few nutrients in iceberg lettuce. Much of the food was fried and as one of my jobs as the Public Health and Sanitation Inspector, I was able to see that the fats used were trans-fats. Most of the food was processed. There was an abundance of processed desserts and many of us found it very difficult to muster up the will-power to just say "no"! Was it any wonder that many of us developed problems with our cholesterol and triglyceride levels?

Meanwhile, at home, we found out that there was a lot more to hydroponic gardening than we realized and ours pretty much gave up the ghost before it ever got off the ground (no pun intended).

Little by little, we got farther and farther away from our good eating style; we would occasionally eat meat and I went back to being the Dessert Queen.

Two years into this new lifestyle and my tumor markers started to rise. With each jump, I would be advised to come back to the US and get a CT scan. In late 2011, a tumor was seen on my CT scan and surgery was planned for early in 2012.

CHAPTER 4

THE "C" WORD

I was lucky this time – the doctor was able to perform my surgery by the da Vinci method – a robotic, laparoscopic device that found not just the golf-ball sized tumor that was seen on CT scan but a second golf ball and about four little mini tumors not visible with the naked eye. This news did not fill me with joy! Instead of believing I had one small tumor, I had six! Geez! The good news is that I could be back to work in two weeks! On my post-operative visit to clear me for travel back to Antigua, the nurse practitioner handed me a stack of medical journal articles on GCT as I was leaving, saying that she knew I liked to keep abreast of my disease.

It was about two weeks later when I finally picked up that stack of articles and started to leaf through them. One word kept popping up here and there – one word that had never been associated with my GCT before and that word was CANCER – Ovarian Cancer to be precise! Wait! Cancer?? Would you believe I had to Google it to find out that my GCT I'd now had for eleven years and three surgeries was actually a rare form of ovarian cancer (less than 2% of all Ovarian Cancers)?

I dove back into that pile of papers and fished out my histology report on the latest tumors.

There was that phrase I'd read before but hadn't really taken in…..that my lymph system had now been invaded. Oh God! I knew what that meant – trouble! Now I knew I had the "C" word *and* that it had invaded my lymph system. Big Trouble!

Semantics! How can that one word change so much in a person's world? On the one hand, I knew this was the same disease I had been dealing with for the past eleven years. But now it seemed so much more sinister, something that sparked so much more fear and I felt a powerlessness and hopelessness creeping into my psyche.

I kept trying to give myself a good shake, a slap in the face and to tell myself over and over until I finally could hear and believe, that nothing had changed! It's the same disease that I'd had my ups and downs with before. I can do this!

Once I faced the ugly truth that I had cancer, I needed to break it to the rest of my family. There was much shock and my brother just point blank said he refused to believe it! End of subject! From my sisters and husband, I got that strong assurance that they are there for me; from my kids I got links to books, articles, and movies.

……..And that's where the next BIG learning comes in!

CHAPTER 5

NO STONE LEFT UNTURNED!

And that's exactly what I did! As I look back, I realize once again, that there are no coincidences in life – certain books or articles just seem to fall into your lap – just when you need them.

I knew one of my fellow a cappella singers, who had recently been diagnosed with breast cancer, had been treated in a Swiss Clinic with alternative methods, the same clinic that enabled her husband to live ten more years happily and healthily, when our local medical institutions could do no more for him and his rare type of cancer. I asked her about this facility and she told me that it would cost $25,000 for starters, but that the doctor who ran the clinic had written a book and she happened to have a copy she could loan me. I excitedly borrowed her book and right away ordered my own copy from Amazon. The book is *The Swiss Secret to Optimal Health* by Dr. Thomas Rau.

In his book, Dr. Rau explains that the type of medicine practiced at the Paracelsus Clinic is biological medicine, a newer vision where the physician "treats the *patient* that has the disease rather than the *disease* that has the patient," a statement of Dr. William Osler, one of the founding fathers of modern medicine.

Dr. Rau believes we need to detoxify our body, to de-acidify the internal environment and he feels his Swiss detox diet will do those two things, as well as help us develop proper intestinal flora.

Once again, it was time to get out the shopping list as we were about to embark on a three week detox diet.

Basically, you start every day with ½ teaspoon of an alkalizing powder, such as baking soda, in an eight ounce glass of warm water. After drinking this, the next course is some broth from a special alkalizing soup made with zucchini, green beans, celery and carrots. The third course each morning was a tablespoon of pure flaxseed oil with your breakfast. The rest of the diet was basically an elimination diet to rule out allergens – starting the first week with a rather strict no meat, no refined sugar, no white flour, no dairy, no nuts except for chestnuts (and you surely can't get those in Antigua), no salt or pepper. You had to drink at least three liters of fluids a day – mostly pure spring water but also broth, herbal teas and unsweetened organic apple juice. Dr. Rau encourages a big breakfast and the main meal to be at lunch time with a lighter meal at dinner. Lunch always has a nice big raw salad with grated vegetables, not just lettuce and included some steamed vegetables. With the evening meal, he believes it is easier on your system to have just your steamed vegetables. No fruit is eaten after 4:00 pm, as he feels it ferments in your gut and stresses the liver.

In Week Two, you can gradually incorporate small amounts of whole grains and goat or sheep cheese.

For Week Three, you finally get to eat a piece of fish and what an exciting night that is! You also get to enjoy a few desserts like his Maple Pecan cookies or Lemon Tart. Let me warn you here, his idea of a dessert is a bit different than mine! I think we tried two different desserts – the first was "Irene's Famous Lemon Tart". For flour, you must use spelt flour – in this case, it called for organic white spelt flour but the best we could do was regular spelt flour. The sweetener was ¼ to ¹/₃ cup of mild honey. The recipe made a small tart, which in my world would have served four to six people....but Dr. Rau suggested it serve ten to twelve! Very small portions!! And not very sweet, but if you haven't had any sweets in three weeks, you still celebrated!

The second recipe we tried was the Maple-Pecan cookies. According to the recipe, you were to reap two dozen cookies out of one cup of spelt flour and 1 cup of pecan halves! Sweetener this time was ¼ cup of maple syrup. Again, we were thrilled that we got to eat a treat but we could easily have eaten a dozen each! For some of the other recipes, ingredients were hard to come by – like fresh figs, chestnut honey, goat yogurt, popped amaranth, to name a few.

The Maintenance Diet is very similar to your third week on the detox diet along with the occasional addition of free-range chicken and healthy fish two or three times a week.

Dr. Rau feels that once you've spent a couple of months eating this way, you can then have the occasional treat without paying the price for it. He does encourage you to continue to avoid refined sugar, white flour, cow dairy products, other than small amounts of organic butter, and cream from time to time, meat, especially pork, shellfish or bottom feeders, processed foods, onions (as he feels this can cause a thickening of the lymph fluids and would prefer us to season with leek, garlic or chives instead), ordinary table salt – instead we should use sea salt or Himalayan salt.

The next chapter of his book is devoted to the Liver Cleanse and here I must admit that I was a naughty girl and have not yet done the Liver Cleanse, although he highly recommends it as it purifies both the liver and the gallbladder. It requires dedicating some free time to being able to cleanse in a way that sounds somewhat similar to a prep for a colonoscopy, but goes a step further, by having to drink (in addition to the Epsom salt solution) a concoction of ¾ cup fresh squeezed grapefruit juice with ½ cup olive oil. I have met several folks who have done this Liver Cleanse and do speak highly of it so I will get to it…one day very soon, I promise!

After completing the three week detox diet, both my husband and I had lost about 5-10 lbs. between us. We both just felt better, lighter and healthier and we became advocates of the alkalizing dietary practices. My husband had one pretty dramatic result.

At times in the past, he had noticed some adverse symptoms when he had dairy products, nothing with any kind of regularity that he could pinpoint to lactose intolerance, though. After completing the detox however, it became clear that he truly was lactose intolerant. Now, whenever he attempted dairy, the unpleasant symptoms let him know, in no uncertain terms, that this was not a good idea!

Little by little, we relaxed our dietary practices but kept rigid about dairy and meat.

The second book I happened upon during this rather intense learning phase was, *Killing Cancer Not People* by Robert G. Wright. This book states right in the first paragraph, written by reviewers, that it is an amazing source of information for anyone researching the definitive relationship that nutrition bears upon our health. It tells what many people have done to heal their cancers naturally and it exposes the "real truth about conventional cancer treatments."

The first strong Do's and Don'ts come in chapter three and they are to STOP eating sugar immediately; STOP eating meat and dairy but he allows an exception for organic cottage cheese if you are on the *Budwig* protocol. He also strongly recommends that we STOP eating packaged foods, trans fats, black pepper, peanuts, cashews, corn, coffee, refined foods, products with yeast, eggs, alcohol, soy foods unless fermented, white rice, white potatoes, fruits except fresh lemons, limes or avocados.

He encourages you to avoid tap water that contains fluoride and/or chlorine. He tells you to do no cooking on aluminum or chemically coated pots and pans but rather to use glass, ceramic or specially made stainless steel cookware.

He advises us to check out our toothpaste for dangerous ingredients and at all costs, to avoid aspartame! And not just toothpaste, but all our cosmetics, lotions and deodorants likely have harmful, carcinogenic ingredients.

His admonitions were overwhelming! It seemed like I would have to make many more drastic changes in my life.

When we got into the products he did advocate, one of the first was apricot seeds or kernels that are inside the seed. These seeds are very high in B-17, also known as amygdalin or Laetrile, and B-15, also known as pangamic acid. So this was the first product I ordered – and while I was at it – I doubled the order!! When the seeds arrived and I read all the warnings on the label, I put the seeds away in the cupboard and finally, two years later, threw them out. I know, I know! I am a coward and a wastrel!!

My only problem with this book was that there were SO many suggestions that I became overwhelmed! I was turning down the corners of so many pages and ordering so many things as I went along!

Actually, in looking through it again now, 3 years later, and as someone who has just completed an Integrative Nutrition Health Coach Certification program, I see so much that resonates with my recent training. I think I need to go back and read this book again!

I'd been hesitant to really do much searching for books on cancer. I think I just didn't want to "own" the disease. I was afraid that if I put much emphasis on that word, the disease would worsen. I also was reluctant to join any kind of support group, but one day I found a group on an Ovarian Cancer website with my specific disease and it was SO nice to be able to exchange notes with those going through the same things. That was the first week on the group site. The second week things had changed. I was reading more and more entries about those losing their battle with the disease and I started wondering how my demise would come about. Would it be my liver, my lungs, would I have metastasis to the bones and would they start crumbling? I quit going to that site – decided that maybe I wasn't ready for that just yet.

One day, while looking for books about dealing with cancer, I came across a book that struck a different tone, one that was truly unique, *Crazy, Sexy Cancer Tips*, by Kris Carr. I downloaded it and started to read it immediately. Kris has a way of writing about a very serious subject but in a way that gives you sound advice in a humorous way.

One suggestion she makes early on is that we cancer *survivors* (and she says we should change the word, *patient*, with survivor – even from the moment we are diagnosed), should have our 'posse'; a support group of other cancer survivors, or friends, or professionals that can help keep us on track, give us practical tips or share their valuable learning.

I knew that this was one Sister that I wanted to keep close! Her conclusion is just too good not to include here, so here goes:

"By completing this book you have officially graduated from Cancer Babe to Cancer Cowgirl. Yee haw! Cancer Cowgirls are a divine order, a free-spirited bunch of powerful women who take charge as they gallop through life's obstacle course. We don't whisper, we ROAR! This is just the beginning, a match to the tinder of curiosity, possibility, and tenacity we all possess. You are complete now. You are whole now. For God's sake, you're a Cancer Cowgirl! A heavenly creature full of sass and fireworks. A dazzling warrior full of peace and fury.

Cancer Cowgirls past and present are survivors. Take the best and leave the rest. Don't forget to feel the ground beneath you and notice the groovy scene as you hitchhike down the highway of one-day-at-a-time. Remember, too, that you are not alone. Your posse is waiting for you. Connect, share, and pen your own tips. She signs it "Peace, veggies, and a lot of glitter, Kris"

Next on my list in this Intensive Learning Phase was what I will call the Wheatgrass Phase of Life. My wonderful kids sent me some information about Ann Wigmore's work with cancer and the healing effects of wheatgrass juice. So once again (what would I do without you, beloved Amazon.com), we found that we could order a kit for growing the wheat and barley grass and then of course, we had to procure an auger-type juicer. We started small, with a hand-crank model. The wheat grass grew beautifully and what a shock when you take that first sip of that intensely green juice! One thing I quickly learned – Do Not Drink Your Wheatgrass Juice Shortly Before You Hope to Go to Bed!! You will NOT sleep!! At least, it surely had that effect on me! Wheatgrass juice energized me! I felt Healthy!! Anybody who can down a shot of that stuff HAS to be healthy! Look at all those chlorophyll-stuffed phytonutrients!!

But one day, we learned another lesson that closed down our wheatgrass operation after several months and that was that it develops mold way too easily! This mold is hard to keep out of the grass that you juice and the last thing a person who is trying to pump up their immune system needs is to be imbibing moldy wheat grass juice! A very knowledgeable Health Food store proprietor advised me that I would be better off buying wheatgrass tablets from a reputable firm. And so, our grass farming days came to an end.

Coincidentally, about the same time we ended our wheatgrass production, my son strongly advised that I get and watch the DVD by Joe Cross of *Fat, Sick and Nearly Dead*. The DVD sat on my shelf for a few months before I finally decided to watch it and when I did, I immediately watched it a second time! Back to Amazon.com, and a couple of weeks later, a beautiful Omega juicer arrived and we started the next phase of our lives – the Juice phase – which is ongoing to this day!

When I think about all I had learned up to this point – that the fruits and vegetables are the most nutrient dense foods and that, by juicing, you can consume so much more than you could if you sat down and tried to eat them – it all makes so much sense! Isn't it true, that 'you are what you eat'? When you juice, you are consuming live foods and lots of them!

Less than two weeks was all it took before people were commenting on how good and how young we were looking! We didn't do the Ten-Day Reboot that Joe Cross recommended (read wimps here!), but we did have our juice before lunch and dinner, twice a day for a whole year before we cut back to just once a day. Our mainstay recipe will have a green apple, some beet, carrots, kale and/ or spinach, cucumber, celery, ginger, and the juice of a lime. The juices are surprisingly delicious! (And this from someone who NEVER eats beets!)

We were still new to the juicing scene when the next learning opportunity dropped into my lap – something I'd never heard of before!

CHAPTER 6

TURNING OVER MORE STONES – IRIDOLOGY AND A MEDICAL INTUITIVE

While visiting a good friend one day, she casually mentioned that she had made an appointment to get her iris read. My eyebrows went up in amazement and I wanted to know more! When I mentioned this to my sister later, she said, "Oh yes, an iridologist, you haven't heard of them?" Never have! I Googled iridology, and after a little research, decided to make an appointment to see this fellow.

I was amazed! When I first went in, I was asked to fill out a medical history form but rather than taking the form, the Iridologist and Herbalist, told me to just turn it over and hold on to it. This fellow then spent at least twenty minutes gazing into one eye with what looked like a jeweler's magnifying glass. He would stop every few minutes and write something down and then go back to gazing. At the end, he took just a quick look into my other eye and then we talked. It was incredible! He was able to tell me about my ovarian cancer disease but went on to mention other organs or systems that needed cleansing or support.

He started with a whole list of supplements to boost my immune system, a regimen for colon and kidney cleansing, treatments to detoxify the body from heavy metals and finished with a thorough list of dietary do's and don'ts.

He ended our consultation by saying that if he'd met me six months earlier, he would have told me not to have that surgery. I told him if I'd met him six months earlier, I wouldn't have listened to him!

So let's start with the immune boosting. I was to take a colloidal silver product, olive leaf extract, as directed on the product, as well as cayenne capsules. I was also to take Fish Oil twice daily with meals. Next, was the colon cleanse. There was no one doing colonic irrigations on our island (and at that point I was very grateful for that fact) which would have been his first choice, so we had to make do with a product called "Super Colon Cleanser, with Psyllium". I was directed to use the product for nine consecutive days a month, for five months. I was also to mix and drink Bentonite Clay twice daily. Then, there was a particular kidney cleanser tea that I was to use three times daily for three months and I was to drink as much young coconut water as possible.

Here is his list of food Do's and Don'ts:

DON'TS

- No white flour, pasta or white bread

- No white rice

- No white sugar

- No dairy products

- No fried foods

- And for me in particular, no soy or edamame

DO NOT eat and drink at the same time, drink a minimum of ½ hour after meals and twenty minutes before meals.

DO'S

- Eat lots of green leafy vegetables daily

- Eat spelt or whole wheat flour when necessary

- Bread should only be spelt flour or seven grain, but don't eat often, follow with heavenly salad. Flour and liquid forms a paste, he reminds us, and we don't want pasty colons!

- Grains: quinoa, amaranth, spelt, kamut, wild rice, brown rice, or teff (never heard of some of these)

- Pasta should be made with spinach or spelt flour

- Sea vegetables: kombu, wakame, arame, hijiki, Irish Sea moss, dulse, kelp, agar agar, and nori (never heard of most of these!)

- Organic chicken or wild fish

Food was to be prepared by steaming, sautéing, baking, boiling, or roasting.

Acceptable sugar substitutes were: raw agave nectar, organic honey, dates, or organic maple syrup.

Acceptable milk substitutes were coconut, almond or rice milk.

I was encouraged to drink ½ of my body weight in ounces of water daily, but could include young coconut water in that total.

Most of all, this fellow pushed his "Heavenly Salad" which did not sound very appealing to me for several reasons but has become a family favorite and has been adopted by many friends who have eaten at our table.

Heavenly Salad

- Green uncooked papaya, with skin – a pie wedge size slice - grated

- Beet – ½ medium sized beet, grated – add more to suit your taste

- Raw pumpkin – small wedge, grated

- Turmeric – piece the size of a small finger, grated

- Carrots – two or three, or more, to suit your taste, grated

- Garlic – one clove, grated or minced

- Other items that can be added as you like are celery, avocado, cucumber, peel and all, chopped or grated

- Other optional herbs are rosemary or thyme

- Dress salad with some cayenne pepper, lime juice and cold pressed olive oil, add sea salt to taste.

I actually ate this salad twice a day for a year! What was truly amazing is that I don't eat beets – ever! But I could handle them in this salad or in our juices. I was also scared to eat the raw, green papaya, especially the skin! We were always told here in the Caribbean that you had to be careful when peeling or preparing green papaya, as the sap would burn your skin – you only cooked green papaya. But we found out that there were no deleterious effects from preparing and eating the salad as recommended.

Some other recommendations this fellow made were to not use yeast and avoid eating yeast breads. When using baking soda or powder, to make sure it was aluminum free. He encouraged me to wash our vegetables with a white vinegar and water solution prior to using. He encouraged the eating of LIVE food with each meal – meaning something like fruits and vegetables that were fresh and local.

On another note, he encouraged massage and chiropractic adjustments regularly, and encouraged a deep breathing practice.

The only down side to this experience was the lack of follow-up. When someone tells you that you have cancer and you start a regimen like the above, you want follow-up! You want to be assured that you are on the right track, that improvements are being made. This iridologist doesn't give you a 'next appointment' but he does give you his phone number and Skype contact info (he travels on and off island a lot). I believe that most of us are looking for fast "cures"! These methods are slow but sure, gradually improving the body's immune system, gradually detoxifying, and then building up good flora and fauna in the gut.

I did contact him about six months later, at which point he said I still had work to do and he gave me a handful of weeds which I was supposed to steep like a tea and then use in an enema. Well....I guess I was getting a bit disenchanted with some of the treatments and maybe he was getting disenchanted with me and my doubts as well, as the next time I called him, he never returned my call, nor did he answer my email. I guess that was also a form of guidance!

My next adventure was two months later. I had a phone consultation with a Medical Intuitive! Up until this time, I had never heard of a Medical Intuitive and couldn't imagine how this person could help but she came highly recommended and had been used by my son and daughter-in-law for a serious issue with their toddler.

They had learned of this woman from one of their friends who spoke highly of her.

It took six weeks to get an appointment and I was excited and didn't know what to expect!

When that day finally arrived and I placed my call and this lovely sounding woman gently asked how she could help me. I just burst out into tears! Here was someone genuinely focused on listening to me—for a whole hour! I had never experienced anything like that before! Frequently, when you are in a doctor's office you are herded in and out so quickly your head spins, you forget to ask your questions. You sometimes feel your doctor is listening to you with one ear and has his hand on the door knob, ready to get to the next patient. (I must say here that I am lucky and this generalization does not include my doctors!)

This woman, however, had given me an hour of her time, to discuss whatever I wanted and I suddenly became speechless and overwhelmed with tears! To get us over this awkward beginning, she told me a bit about herself, of how she was born with what we might think were disabilities, but in training with a surgeon, became her abilities!

The first thing she said she could tell about me was that electrically – I was switched off! I was baffled by this but she briefly equated it to my 'chi' or 'Qi'. A dictionary defines it as:

"A strong life force (chi) makes a human being totally alive, alert and present while a weak force results in sluggishness and fatigue. You can increase and develop your chi to overcome illness, become more vibrant and enhance mental capacity."

She felt this had been turned off since the age of eight – and that she felt that something really stressful had happened to me about that time. (At the time of this consultation, I had no clue what this could have been! Even today, I'm not absolutely sure but have some possibilities. I also wonder if whatever happened also prevented that spirit of Starry Jones to surface now and again.)

She spoke a bit about my lineage – on my father's side, there was a propensity to liver issues, sometimes due to alcohol and as for me, I developed the first cyst on my liver at age eight. On my mother's side, the women had blood sugar issues, problems with weak pancreas, and as it relates to me, I had blood sugar problems since conception; that my cancer was a sugar-fed cancer.

This was all very interesting to me as all my CT scans have reported cysts on my liver. When I was pregnant, I was what they call a gestational diabetic – basically I developed diabetes while pregnant but after delivery, my blood sugar problem reverted back to normal. I was always told that there was an increased chance that I would become diabetic later in life. None of this information had been reported to the Medical Intuitive ahead of time.

Next came her dietary guidelines. I told her about my consultation with the Iridologist and she felt I was divinely guided to him. So, now for the new and improved dietary guidelines:

- NO flour at all! – no glutens

- Rice is the only acceptable grain for me

- Eliminate all cane products, I can have honey but no other sugars and especially no corn syrup!

- No milk, no dairy

- Coconut is good

- Fruit and vegetables excellent

- Nuts and seeds when you can digest them

- Absolutely no mushrooms, no fungal products, no yeast!

- Focus on chlorophyll-rich foods – green leafy vegetables, green powders, kale, alfalfa, spirulina, and chlorella.

- The perfect diet for me is a vegan diet but with some fish. Goat cheese would also be okay.

At this point, she abruptly shifted the conversation to what she called the visceral and told me that she saw in me a new sadness in the last ten years, though she saw no specific origin or cause. At first, I was stumped because to me in my nursing terminology, visceral had to do with internal organs but when I looked it up, I realized another definition was intuitive feeling or gut feeling rather than intellectual reasoning. She felt that I had a habit of taking on the pain of others; and that I had developed a toxicity I had accumulated from others -- a trait that I needed to lose.

Being a nurse, taking on the pain and suffering of others tends to be very easy but I remembered back to a lecture in Nursing 101, about sympathy versus empathy. To have sympathy for a patient was to understand their feelings or suffering but when you are empathizing with that patient, you are actually taking on and feeling their pain and suffering. I guess I have a tendency to do the latter and she was telling me I needed to keep this in check!

As to the new sadness in the past ten years, the only thing I can think of was that our family had been amazingly blessed all my life. We had been spared the tragedies that so many of our friends and colleagues had suffered. But in those past ten years, we had faced three surgeries and a cancer diagnosis for me, a liver transplant for my husband, the death of my beloved father and the death of both my husband's parents. Maybe it was that uncomfortable feeling that anything can happen to anyone, at any moment!

But back to our consultation. Once again, she asked me about something that had happened in my childhood and suddenly memories came flooding back to me of being molested by an old man (seemed like he was at least 80, in my eyes at that time), a man that my father had taken pity on since his wife had recently died and he was alone and so brought him home to dinner one evening. The old man took an interest (to say the least) in me and my sisters – something we never talked about, even with each other, until recently. The Medical Intuitive said I should forgive my father. Forgive my father?? I was adamant that I did not blame my father – in my eyes he could do no wrong but she felt he should have protected us and I needed to forgive him.

Next she advised me to focus on the blessings, that the blessings are limitless; and that I am meant to get over this, to grow and to wake up to God's plan.

Well, all I can tell you is that I was well and truly blown away by this consultation. I felt I had learned so much, things I wanted to share and some that I just wanted to keep close to me for a while.

I had a subsequent consultation when my markers had shot up and surgery was scheduled. (The Intuitive had told me in our first consultation that I would never have to undergo that type of surgery again). I was pretty depressed at the time. Her advice was that I needed to lose the stressors in my life....or needed to learn how to deal with them.

I knew that one of my big stressors was my job but I wasn't ready to walk away from that stressor just at this point – the benefits were outweighing the stressors, in my eyes.

Another stressor was at home. My dear husband was home alone all day, so would frequently listen to the local radio station belonging to the opposition party of the government. There were hot topics every day and my husband couldn't wait for me to get home so he could share them. And when he did so, he got just as excited or agitated as the folks that were calling in to voice their complaints. After listening to everybody's complaints all day in my clinic, the last thing I wanted to hear when I got home was anything of a negative nature.

About that time, I believe it was Oprah, who was encouraging folks to every day, list at least three things that we were grateful for that day. I suggested to my husband that when I got home and we sat down to dinner, this should be our topic of conversation. We would share with each other the three things we were grateful for this day. And you know? It worked! This became our nightly pattern. He was particularly happy when I came to realize the next step, which was expressing gratitude to him for all that he did for me and for us rather than walking in the door and immediately finding fault with the things he had or hadn't done that day!

Recognizing all the things I am grateful for has become an important practice in my life now, whether it is the great parking spot that just opened up right in front of the building I needed to visit or the breath-taking cloud formations!

I had one last consultation with this lovely woman about a year later and she was very pleased with the progress I was making. My "electrical problems" were no longer there. She was happy that I was making plans for my future; I was going back to school to become a Health Coach. She did however, encourage me to stay in touch with my doctor, and that I was blessed to have her on my team!

CHAPTER 7

THE HOMEOPATHY I NEVER KNEW!

Continuing on this journey of leaving no stone unturned, I met an Irish Homeopathic physician on a trip to Israel in 2011. We quickly developed a warm friendship and I filed her contact information away, in the event I ever needed it. I had been trying all these wonderful new practices in my life like Qi Gong, going gluten free, vegetable juicing, healthy superfoods, raw salads and yet my tumor markers continued to slowly rise.

I decided it was time for Homeopathy! I contacted Fran and we set up a time for a Skype consultation. What I understood about Homeopathy at that time was that it was a science that believed in giving you microscopic amounts of a chemical formula that would treat your illness. We had used homeopathic remedies years earlier when either one of us or our children were sick. We consulted this lovely older Chinese woman who had a health shop in town. We found the remedies to be safe and effective on many occasions.

Prior to the consultation, Fran wanted me to send her a brief history of my illness. Then, in the next email, she asked different questions – questions that surprised me! Who is Linda and what makes her tick? Do I have recurring dreams or nightmares?

There were other questions but quite frankly, I couldn't get past the first one. I wrote back that as soon as I found out who Linda was and what made her tick, I would let her know. Somehow, I think I played right into her hands. I had no idea that in homeopathy, they also want to dig into your psyche!

During our Skype consultation she again asked me that question and I described myself as a malleable lump of clay....I could mold myself into whatever a situation dictated. I guess that I could be described as a people pleaser. And yes, I had a recurring nightmare – it was of a tidal wave approaching – sudden, huge waves that were terrifying, but I always woke up at the last moment.

Fran was an experienced super sleuth! She knew how to dig and she brought things out of me that made my eyes pop when I realized what I had just said. She asked a lot of questions about my early childhood and my relationship with my parents and the biggest epiphany for me was when I said that I really only felt loved when I was sick! Oh My! Did I just say that??

After our 90 minute consultation, I was exhausted! Fran was going to mail me the remedies she thought would best suit me. In the meantime, one of the skeletons that slipped out of my closet while talking to Fran, was the fact that there had been a serious "oops!" moment in my life, when I was nearing my last year of high school. I had gotten pregnant.

I had to go away to a home for unwed mothers and had to give up the baby for adoption. Fran thought this was a pretty significant skeleton! She wondered if I had ever tried to find my son. I told her that years ago, I had made an attempt but soon felt that it would be like finding a needle in a haystack!

After our consultation, I must admit that my thoughts kept drifting back to my big revelation – it had been buried for so many years! There were no secrets in my family, I had told my kids about this chapter in my life – it was meant to be a very strong birth control lecture! About twenty years earlier, I had written to the adoption agency to give them permission to open my records should anyone (like my son) ever want to find me. Maybe ten years ago, I caught a show on TV about adoptees being reunited with their birth parent/s and I wrote to the organization but found that the price was more than I could pay at that time. Maybe now was the time to try again.

CHAPTER 8

NEEDLE IN A HAYSTACK

Two weeks later, my relief nurse flew in to Antigua from Chicago so that I could fly south to cover the base at Ascension Island. Just before I left, she pulled me aside with a very serious look on her face, said she had something she wanted to share with me and told me, "There's a man in my life!" Well, I really didn't know what to say. Maryann is a year older than me, is a fabulous nurse and has done a significant amount of traveling as a nurse, all over the world. Still, I didn't think it would be such a big deal that she had a boyfriend. Without further explanation, Maryann handed me her computer and insisted I read a certain email. I thought her behavior a little strange but I could see this was very important to her.

A few lines into the email and I felt the tears start to prick my eyes then they just started streaming down my face...maybe not the reaction she was expecting....but when I finished the email, I looked up at her and told her she had NO idea how this email had affected me....you see, this was not an email from a suitor, this was an email from her son....a son she had given up for adoption maybe a year after I had given up mine and he had searched and found his mother! We wept together when I told her my story.

I knew at that moment that this was no accident, I was meant to find my son!

As soon as I got back from Ascension, I started looking around the internet for guidance, for registries, for agencies and it was all feeling rather futile….and costly! On a Friday afternoon in April, I registered yet one more time, on a site called Findmyfamily.org. They asked for the birth place and date and fortunately there was a place to leave comments. I could no longer remember the date, just knew it was in August, 1965, in southern California. Three hours later, my iPad dinged with an incoming email and to my shock, it was from this website owner – she said she found the exact date my son was born. She asked me if I had any other information, like his adopted name or date of adoption. I wrote back immediately letting her know I had no other information but that I was seeking any information I could get, that I wanted to find my son and could she possibly help? Then there was nothing!

Three days went by and there was no word from Judy, my "Search Angel". Late Monday afternoon, I wrote her one more time asking her if she could at least give me the name of a reputable agency that might be able to help me. By the time I got home, there was an email from Judy and she was asking if she could call me, "We need to talk!" Even writing this now, I get all choked up!

I called Judy right away and she suggested that I might want to get a pen and paper and sit down. She had found my son!!

I grabbed a pen and paper, climbed up on my bed, hands shaking with nervousness, and asked her to go on. And that she did….she seemed to go on and on describing my son as someone very important, someone I would be very proud of.

Finally, I cut into her conversation and said, "Can you at least tell me his name??" I was beginning to think this might be a scam, that she was going to ask for a large sum of money before telling me anything and so I asked her that. She said, "You can make a donation on my website or you can just pay it forward." Not the words of a scam artist! Finally, Judy told me his name and I just kept repeating it over and over in my head, trying it on for size. Then she said she had another big surprise for me….she said that she saw on my registration form for her site that I was a nurse – she was so tickled to be able to tell me that my son was also in the medical field, a well-respected surgeon!

At this point, my head was reeling and I was laughing and crying! I asked if she could tell me where he was and when she did, I nearly fell off the bed! He was living and practicing maybe fifteen miles from where I used to live, in Virginia! I sat there just absolutely dazed! Finally, I asked if she had a picture and she said all she had was a small thumbnail one but she emailed me the picture. As soon as

I could pull it up, doubts arose. I was looking for any sign of familiarity and didn't see them in that tiny picture.

But despite those first doubts, I right away emailed my kids to tell them what just happened. In less than fifteen minutes, my daughter-in-law had found the website for my surgeon son's group of doctors – a treasure trove – as there was not only his curriculum vitae but also a big picture, and when that picture opened up, I saw my old boyfriend! I started to cry! What's more, I saw the family dimple, he had the same teeth, the same ears!! He was handsome and he looked so much like my younger son, his half-brother! What an absolute miracle!! To find my son who was given up for adoption nearly 48 years earlier and to find him so quickly!

Judy, the Search Angel, (and what an angel she was to me now!!) asked me if I knew what I wanted to do now. Of Course!! Judy explained that frequently, in these situations, one has an intermediary person make the first contact. I asked Judy if she would be my intermediary and contact him on my behalf and she said to give her a little time to find the right words but that she would be happy to do it.

From that moment on, I made absolutely sure that my cell phone and iPad were always in reach! An interminable two weeks went by and Judy had been unable to contact him due to her own issues at home, so I decided to take matters back into my own hands and I wrote him a letter. It took nearly a week – it had to be perfect and I do believe it truly was.

I included the story leading up to his conception, that we were high school sweethearts, both from well-respected homes, both honor students and that it was during the Cuban missile crisis, with practice drills for atomic bomb blasts, and all the fear these drills instilled. Anyway, I got pregnant. Telling our parents was the hardest thing we had ever had to do. I'd had no choice but to go away to the Salvation Army Home for Unwed Mothers and to give the baby up for adoption. I included pictures of his father, his grandparents (my parents) and of his two half-siblings, my son and daughter. The letter went certified and registered and from the moment it was signed for by his wife, I lived in constant anticipation that I would hear from him any minute!

Six long weeks went by and not a word! It was agonizing, trying to second guess all the possibilities! I decided I had to have one more try so I sent the same letter to his office but in a confidential, for your eyes only, envelope. Three days later, I finally got the email I'd been waiting for! I was so excited, laughing, crying, yet too afraid to open the email and actually read it…my sister yelled at me to "READ IT!" It was a nice response, kind of reserved, hesitant – said he wanted to get excited but that he hoped I would understand that he would have to do his own search before he could really allow himself to be excited. That was not quite the joyous response I was hoping for, but I could muster a bit more patience and await his search results.

Two weeks later, he sent me an email asking if I would be willing to do a DNA test. There was no question in my mind, of course I was willing! Four days later, I received an email from my son with the subject line that I had better check the DNA lab site, the results were in. I started ranting and raving that I KNEW that he was my son, maybe the test type we used wasn't correct, etc., etc....I hadn't actually read the email, just the subject heading. When I opened the email, it said, "You had better check the website as the results are in, MOM!!!" And of course, I didn't need to read any further as I was skipping and screaming and crying and laughing and dancing and soon everybody else in the family was joining in! Joy, oh joy!! A few days later, I got the email that my son was coming to Antigua in four weeks!

I have to interject here that two weeks later, I had my routine tumor markers drawn and unfortunately, the results had taken a significant jump. My Florida oncologist wanted me to come in for a CT scan to look for tumors. A week later, I was able to make a quick trip, had the CT scan done, and got the dreaded news that I had another tumor and needed surgery. I told her there was absolutely no way I could have surgery now, and proceeded to tell her my miraculous story of finding my son and his upcoming trip to Antigua. Honestly, I didn't care if it was going to kill me – I was not missing that August 20th reunion! Fortunately, my doctor agreed that we had some time and scheduled the surgery for two months later.

Two weeks later, my son arrived in Antigua and I met him for the second time in our lives, the day before his 48th birthday!

I still was not exactly sure what to expect from him. A dream that turned into more of a nightmare a couple of weeks before his arrival, had me meeting him on a big yacht and when he introduced me to his wife and I reached out my hand to shake hands with her, she turned on her heel and walked away! My wise daughter advised me to envision the reunion the way I wanted it to happen and to write it all down and just keep that in my focus.

When the day actually came, he drove out to our house but had let me know that he only wanted to meet me this visit, no other family. Meanwhile, my 91 year old mother had said to me, "Oh, I wish I could be a fly on the wall of this reunion!" I hoped I could persuade my son to at least come meet my Mom, his Grand-mom! For me, I wanted to touch him, hold his hand, something I had never been able to do from the moment he was born. In the Home for Unwed Mothers, we were allowed to hold the baby one time, to feed him one time and to dress the baby but I knew if they ever placed that beautiful baby in my arms, I would *never* let go!

When my handsome son arrived that momentous day, I was a nervous wreck! As he got out of his car and came over to me, he grabbed me up in such a tight hug I thought I would burst with joy!!

Even now, two years later, the tears spring to my eyes just relating the story. My husband took our picture together and then left us alone. We talked and talked and talked, just looking at each other and grinning! Finally it was time for lunch and my sister, who was looking after my Mom, had made us a lovely pasta. My wonderful son was now willing to walk down to the other house to meet one of my sisters and my Mom.

It was a wonderful luncheon! My sister had lots of questions but one she asked was if his wife was onboard and excited with all this. He said that actually, she was not. Uh Oh! There was my dream! But when I stopped to think about it, he had not yet told his adoptive mother about being reunited with his birth mother. And I can fully understand his wife being loyal to his adoptive mother. Given time and opportunity, I knew all these little glitches would work out – doesn't love conquer all??

When my son left a few hours later, I fixed a cup of tea, sat out on the gallery (what you folks call a porch) and recognized a strange, unusual feeling that I had never felt before, or at least not in a very long time. I felt replete! Complete! With such a peace I have never known!

I know I went on a bit here, but to me, this was a very significant step back to becoming who I really was, my authentic self.

I could just see my homeopathic physician smiling from across the ocean, not just because she was the catalyst to help me find my son but also that her remedies were helping to restore the original Linda!

And as if this story wasn't miracle enough, what came next, brought about a second big miracle in my life!

CHAPTER 9

TO WHAT DO WE ATTRIBUTE THIS MIRACLE?

As the impending surgery date grew closer, some of that lovely contented spirit brought about by meeting my son, started to weaken and fear started creeping in. I knew from my previous surgery that my lymph system had been invaded. I worried that this was the beginning of the end. I had young grandchildren. I didn't want to be just a picture on the wall; I wanted a place in their lives!

I had another phone consultation with the Medical Intuitive but this time I did not come away from it with an optimistic feeling, rather I learned I must be "content with the Will of God". That can sometimes be difficult when you feel young, healthy and have so much to live for! In a particularly 'down' moment, I wandered into our base library and for some reason, just started tidying the place up. I discovered several boxes of new books that hadn't even been put up on the shelves yet. There on the top was a book that I knew was there just for me! It was called *Proof of Heaven* by Dr. Eben Alexander. The cover stated it was, "A Neurosurgeon's journey into the afterlife". Sounded like just the ticket!

I took the book home and started reading it that night after climbing into bed. I read till the wee hours as I could not put the book down.

By page 41, I was a changed person. On this particular page, during his 'near-death' experience, Dr. Alexander said he was given a message that he says, ran something like this: "You are loved and cherished, dearly, forever." That statement alone started the tears. But he went on, "You have nothing to fear." Basking in the glow of being loved and cherished, I started to lose the fear. Then he adds, "There is nothing you can do wrong." He goes on to say that the message flooded him with a vast and crazy sensation of relief, like being handed the rules to a game he'd been playing all his life without ever fully understanding it. Wow! In one instant, I seemed to have lost my fear of death and at the thought of being loved and cherished, dearly and forever, I wept!

I had an intense fear of death since childhood and that prayer many of us were taught and recited nightly to our parents before they kissed us good-night and turned out the light, "Now I lay me down to sleep, I pray the Lord my soul to keep. If I should die before I wake...???!!! Of course with my parents, I finished the prayer and then when the lights were off, I'd go back to that line, "If I should die before I wake??" and the fear started to creep in and any sleepiness vanished! I would lay there and start imagining what death was like, and as the minutes and hours ticked away and one by one the lights went out in the house and now my parents were going to bed too! And I was all alone, in the total darkness, and imagining what eternity was like in this blackness and aloneness.

My heart would start pounding and in a flash, I was out of that bed, running down the hall and climbing into my parent's bed – not content to be along the edge but only feeling safe when right in the middle, between the two of them.

Reading Dr. Alexander's book was the first time I truly felt free of those old fears. And wasn't that part of the message he received, that we have *nothing* to fear? I could truly feel my fear of the surgery and the outcome of my disease, slowly slipping away.

Two days later, even before I finished reading Dr. Alexander's book, a Facebook link from a friend connected me to a TV interview of a woman by the name of Anita Moorjani. In this interview, she was relating her near-death experience and the book she wrote called *Dying to Be Me*. Thanks to Amazon again, one week later, that book was in my hands. In the meantime, I had searched every link to Anita that I could find and watched all the interviews available online. Her story was of her journey from stage four lymphoma cancer, to near death, to true and complete healing.

During her final hospitalization and coma, Anita describes being present in her hospital room, watching everything that was being done to her, intensely feeling her family's grief but not being able to communicate that she was alright, in fact, never better!

She said she had no emotional attachment to her seemingly lifeless body, that it didn't feel like it was hers and instead she felt free, liberated and magnificent! On the one hand, she states she felt a deep pull on her emotions, to the drama that was unfolding around her inert form, but that she also was feeling that attachment start to recede as a grander plan was unfolding. She felt that everything was perfect and going according to plan, that she was surrounded by the reassuring feeling of a greater tapestry unfolding, where everything was exactly as it should be in the grand scheme of things.

Like Dr. Alexander in his book, Anita tries to explain that as she became more deeply enveloped by the other realm, she was surrounded by superb and glorious unconditional love, that our words don't do it justice –" love, joy, ecstasy and awe poured into me, through me, and engulfed me. I was swallowed up and enveloped in more love than I knew existed.....I suddenly knew things that weren't physically possible."

It was when Anita says that she had a choice – to go back to her body or to proceed toward death that she became aware of a new level of truth. She felt that since she discovered who she really was and understood the magnificence of her true self; that if she chose to go back to life, her body would heal rapidly—not in months or weeks, but in days! She knew that the doctors would not be able to find a trace of cancer.

Yet, she was astounded by this revelation and wanted to understand why. "It was then that I understood that my body is only a reflection of my internal state. If my inner self were aware of its greatness and connection with All-That-Is, my body would soon reflect that and heal rapidly." She became aware that she still had a purpose to fulfill in life and that all she had to do to discover this purpose was just to *be herself.* She understood that at the core, our essence is made of pure love. We are pure love – every single one of us. "How can we *not* be if we come from the Whole and return to it? She states that this biggest revelation felt like a bolt of lightning, that she understood that merely by being the love she truly is, she would heal both herself and others; that our only purpose of life is to be our self, live our truth and be the love that we are. She states that, at this point, the spirit of her father communicated to her, "Now that you know the truth of who you really are, go back and live your life *fearlessly.*"

After reading those two books and the joyous reunion with my son, I felt ready for whatever life was going to dish up for me, but somehow, I had an inner, secret knowing that it was all going to work out just fine. A few days before the scheduled surgery, my husband and I flew up to Florida. My doctor wanted to repeat the CT scan just before surgery to see how much the tumor had grown and if there were additional tumors now visible. Being the nosy nurse that I am, I always request a copy of the results and usually get them (and read them) before the doctor sees them.

It was the same this time. As I sat in the car, in the parking lot, I opened the envelope and read through the report. I was perplexed! I read through the report again. The tumor was gone!! I thought maybe I had the wrong report but it all appeared in order. I went back to the hotel room and shared the report with my husband and we both laughed and cried, but then common sense got a hold of us and we decided to save our celebrations till after meeting with the oncologist the following morning.

The next day, we sat in the doctor's office, still with those matching, hopeful grins on our faces. The doctor took the disk of the CT scan and went back into her office. A few minutes later, she called us in. She said she played the scan backwards and forwards and the radiologist was right – there was no trace of the tumor and what's more, she said, everything looked great!! We all stood up and did the 'happy dance' and the doctor kept asking, "What did you do? I have to know what you did!" When I told her about reading those two books, about the meeting of my son, she shook her head and said, "But what did you do?" I could see in her mind, there was no room for something as vague, as ethereal, as transitory emotions aroused by books or reunions that could affect something as tangible as a tumor that was clearly visible just two months earlier. Then I remembered that I was also taking those two homeopathic remedies and that I didn't even know their names, as my homeopathic physician didn't want me to be influenced— she knew I would look them up and read all about them.

My oncologist latched onto that and said she needed to know the names of those remedies. That was something tangible. And who knows, maybe the fantastic results were due to those two homeopathic remedies I had been taking religiously.

Talk about a triumphal return – many folks knew that I was going up to Florida for surgery because my cancer had returned. When the news spread that my tumor had mysteriously disappeared, it was like I had become some kind of local folk hero!

Life was good! I was still flying high in my bubble of happiness when a couple of months later, I went for my annual physical for the company. I proudly showed off my CT scan results to our company doctor fully expecting the same kind of reception I had gotten from everyone else but what I got was a pin to burst my bubble. The doctor said, "Oh, I see that sort of thing all the time – it was just a lymph node that went up and then back down – it doesn't mean a thing!" Try as I might to put a wall up between those words and my heart and soul, I was afraid that I wasn't fast enough and his words were stronger than my defenses. I left that office totally dejected! If there is one lesson that I could convey to every health practitioner who deals with patients, it is to know when to speak and when not to! Choose your words wisely. They carry such a power and no individual should ever have to lose hope over a practitioner's words.

After all, like I've told so many of my patients over the years, there is the physician and then there is the Divine Physician! And guess which one really calls the shots! (No pun intended!)

CHAPTER 10

INTEGRATIVE NUTRITION – COMING HOME TO WHERE I'M SUPPOSED TO BE!

A few months later...surprise, surprise... the tumor markers were rising again. But something was different this time. I wasn't falling completely apart and telling the world. I felt like I just needed more time to get my act back together again, in fact I was bargaining with the oncologist to give me a few more months.

One day, a chance email with a link to an "I Can Do It" conference sponsored by Hay House, ignited a spark within me again. Two of my favorite authors were among the fascinating list of speakers – Kris Carr of *Crazy Sexy Cancer Tips* and Anita Moorjani of *Dying to Be Me*. I called my sister and immediately proposed that the two of us should take a road trip and attend that conference. Less than three weeks later, we were on our way, having a great adventure in the process. We both loved the conference and what a thrill it was for me to see and hear both ladies as speakers and to give Anita a hug and tell her how much her book meant to me. She is just as wonderful in person as she is on paper!

Something happened to me that weekend. I felt the first inkling that I was getting my power back.

I felt like something wonderful was going to happen but I had no clue what it might be.

A few days after getting home, one of my former co-workers, a highly respected nurse practitioner, posted something on Facebook about going back to school, to the Institute of Integrative Nutrition. I thought, "Wait! I know more about nutrition than she does," what with all my previous dietary explorations. I decided I'd better see what she was getting herself into. I clicked on the link to the program and the rest is history! If you had told me a month earlier, that I was going to be going back to school at age sixty-six, I would have told you that you were nuts! But when I read about this program, it resonated so strongly within me that there was no reasoning with me. I was working full-time, and then some! Where was I going to find the time to take this year-long course? The school said it would take between five to eight hours a week – I was already operating on a deficit budget of at least two to three hours a week. Never mind! I was taking this course to become a Health Coach and in one year I was going to retire from my stressful job at the base and become a Health Coach, working as many or as few hours as I wanted. I knew this was the right decision for me.

From the very first lecture, I was hooked. It soon became apparent, a few days into the course, that there were now two of us that were equally passionate. My nightly routine would be to watch or listen to a lecture while my husband

and I ate dinner. My husband became a serious advocate and even found me my first client when after six months we were allowed to start working with real clients and not just classmates. The school's mission is to "play a crucial role in improving health and happiness, and through that process, create a ripple effect that transforms the world".

I certainly wasn't the only student with a two-fold purpose in attending – there were quite a few of us with one disease or another who intended to bring healing to ourselves first and then to others.

During this year of study, we learned so many wonderful things! Early on in the course we studied the importance of self-care – something many of us are deficient in, as somehow we've adopted an attitude over the years that the busier we are, the more important we are. But how can we help care for others if we are so frazzled ourselves? How can we be good listeners, if our heads are full of our "to do" lists and what's next on our schedules?

I learned about a new-to-me field of medicine called Functional Medicine, practiced by doctors like Dr. Frank Lipman and Dr. Mark Hyman, to mention just two.

In this field, the doctor doesn't so much treat the disease as he treats the deficiency in the person that caused them to manifest the disease – getting to the root cause, so to speak. Doesn't that make so much sense?

One of the most unique and important concepts taught in this program is bio-individuality. I always thought that if you wanted to fight cancer or other chronic diseases, you had to eat the same way I ate. I had been vegetarian for many years but now I was starting to have meat cravings. What a relief to know that we are each unique and our bodies have unique requirements. Maybe we just need to listen to our bodies? But on the other hand, if your body is craving sugar and salt, then perhaps there is a deficiency in your diet that is making you think that it is sugar or salt that you need when really, your body might be needing energy and the craving for salt might be due to an inadequate mineral level. Learning how to deconstruct cravings was another aspect of our studies.

Over the course of the first six months, we studied many dietary theories and each week, my poor husband would be so confused as to what groceries to buy and what food to cook this week! The lectures were so good that after each one, I pronounced that we are now vegan, or going Macrobiotic, or Paleo, or GAPS (Gut and Psychology Syndrome). Then there were Zone Diets, Blood Type diets, Ayurvedic diets, Glycemic load diets and High Protein, Mediterranean or South Beach diets….etc., etc.

I must admit that I was confused but then I just started listening to what my body was telling me and I would follow through, in the end becoming much more relaxed about what I eat – not nearly so fanatic!

Basically we all want to eat 'clean'; we want foods that are not processed but prepared in our own kitchens. If we eat meat then we should do our best to find organic, grass-fed meat or free-range chickens that have not been pumped full of additives, hormones or antibiotics. We want to stick with healthy fats like butter from grass-fed cows, olive oil, coconut oil, just to mention a few good oils, not man-made hydrogenated fats and oils.

We want to avoid consuming sugar – it is highly addictive – but instead use healthier sweeteners like honey or maple syrup or ones that contain few to no calories like stevia. We want to eat an abundance of healthy, organic, when possible, fruits and vegetables – the more colorful our diet, the better! And the grains should be whole grains like brown rice, amaranth, millet, barley, kasha, or quinoa or starchy vegetables like pumpkin, sweet potato or other squash.

We need to drink plenty of good quality water to keep our system flushed of toxins and to keep well hydrated.

The school has further developed this nutritional picture by advocating that there are other things that feed us, things that Joshua Rosenthal, the founder, calls Primary Foods; lifestyle factors that create optimal health – such as relationships, career, physical activity and spirituality. What a great opportunity to look deeply into each of these aspects of our lives to see what might need tweaking a bit...or more!

I gained new insights on my relationship with my husband of 35 years – hopefully learning in the process how to better communicate with each other, to express appreciation for each other, the importance of a good, sustaining hug! Who knows? We might even make it another 35 years at this rate!

Unlike many folks, I am fortunate to already be in a career that I love but so many people today are merely in a job to earn a living. The thought of loving what you do might seem like a far off pipe dream! But even loving my career as a nurse, there is such a thing as burn-out!

When it comes to physical activity there is room for improvement. Tennis brings me much joy but work and school didn't leave me much time for tennis or Qi Gong for that matter. But recently, I signed up for a yoga class and I have decided to make that a permanent addition in my new healthy lifestyle, along with frequent walks. The benefits of yoga are numerous and I want to 'walk the talk' of my new health coach self!

Talking about a spiritual practice can be a touchy subject for some folks these days.

There is certainly room for individuality there as well. We learned that encouraging a routine of regular meditation is one way to tip-toe through the potential mine field of talking 'religion'.

As Joshua Rosenthal says in his book, *Integrative Nutrition*, "Developing spiritual openness and sensitivity can add depth and meaning to your life in a way that nourishes you on a profound level."

As a member of the Baha'i Faith, I felt very secure and comfortable in my spiritual practice but after listening to a lecture on meditation, I decided it was time to incorporate this into my daily practice. Fortunately for me, about that same time, Deepak Chopra and Oprah Winfrey were offering a free 21 day guided meditation program. It was a great way to get started!

I cannot speak highly enough of this inspiring Integrative Nutrition program and the wonderful experience of meeting so many like-minded individuals who were also passionate about these studies. This course has SO much to offer you, whether it is to gain knowledge for your own sake or whether it is to take up a new career as an Integrative Nutrition Health Coach.

But my learning didn't stop with this wonderful course. The next phase amplified many of the things I had studied throughout this past year and brought more profound learning that is especially useful for those suffering from any chronic disease or cancer.

CHAPTER 11

MANY PATHS TO HEALING

In the last few months, there were two books that really summarized my personal journey with this disease. The first one was *Mind Over Medicine* by Dr. Lissa Rankin. The cover says, "Scientific Proof That You Can Heal Yourself". I felt that I'd already witnessed this fact when I went back for surgery in 2013 and my tumor had disappeared. I mainly credited this to the changes in my state of mind after reading *Proof of Heaven* and *Dying to Be Me*. Dr. Rankin again affirms the important role our mind plays in our wellness or our illness. We've all heard stories about the placebo effect – people overcoming diseases, believing they were taking an actual medication when in truth, they were taking a 'sugar pill'. The converse is true also and it is sometimes called the *nocebo* effect. Many of us become familiar with this effect when we are in medical school or nursing school and start getting symptoms of the many diseases we study!

Dr. Rankin shares in her book that she had patients who exercised regularly, ate all the right foods, were not overweight, didn't smoke and yet still had one chronic disease or other and conversely, she had patients who ate poorly, exercised rarely, forgot to take their supplements and yet enjoyed good health.

She says this was when she decided that rather than focusing on a traditional medical history questionnaire, she started asking people to tell her about their lives. This then, inspired her to come up with two important, what she calls "mother-lode", questions: "What do you think might lie at the root of your illness?" and "What does your body need in order to heal?" This is quite a far cry from what we've come to know about our traditional medical approach!

The more I read from this book, the more excited I got – I think, mostly the excitement was because I *knew* these things to be true, they resonated within me, especially when Dr. Rankin describes her *Whole Health Cairn*....fortunately she described what a cairn is as I was not familiar with the term. It is those stacks of balanced stones you might see adorning beaches or marking hiking trails or sacred landmarks. So, the foundation of her *Whole Health Cairn*, the bottom rock, if you will, is what she calls 'our inner pilot light' – "that inner knowing, or healing wisdom of our body and soul that knows what's true for you and guides you, in your own unique way, back to better health." Atop this foundation rock, she has the next stone as our work or life purpose and then relationships. Atop those two, she has spirituality. Next comes creativity and sexuality and on top of those is our environment. The next to the last layer is mental health and then money and the very top stone is our physical health.

She surrounds her *Whole Health Cairn* with a "Healing Bubble" of love, gratitude, service and pleasure – especially important is the love and compassion we must have for ourselves!

Dr. Rankin has 'Six Steps to Healing Yourself', which are:

- Step One: Believe you can heal yourself.

- Step Two: Find the right support – not only in friends and family but in your physician, too!

- Step Three: Listen to your body and intuition.

- Step Four: Diagnose the root causes of your illness – and by this, she certainly doesn't mean that you become your one and only physician – absolutely not! But in addition to working with a physician who supports you, you need to ascertain what might be triggering the stress responses that are likely contributing to your illness.

- Step Five: Write the prescription for yourself. If the root cause of your illness is a weakened immune system due to loneliness, job stress, or other depression, the illness may very well come back unless you treat the root cause, or you will end up with another illness.

- Step Six: Surrender attachment to the outcomes. This, to me, is the tricky one!

- We may do everything right, and follow just what she's given us, and yet we may not be cured. As Dr. Rankin says, "Who are we to know what the Universe has in store for us? How can we anticipate what lessons we're here on this earth to learn and what life challenges we need to face in order to learn them? Perhaps some of us are meant to be sick so we can learn what our soul longs to learn and model how to weather illness with grace. The grace comes in fighting until it's time to stop fighting, and appreciating every step of the journey, even when it doesn't go our way." She goes on to say, "But if you do everything within your power to make your body ripe for miracles—and then you let go and trust the journey—you pave the way for peace, serenity, and joy beyond your wildest imagining."

Before I even finished Dr. Lissa Rankin's book, the next one was waiting on my bedside table and that was *Radical Remission* by Kelly A. Turner, Ph.D., which is about surviving cancer against all odds. I had seen an online interview between Kris Carr of *Crazy, Sexy Cancer Tips* and Kelly Turner, where she spoke of her book which, at that time, was about to be released. This book evolved from her dissertation research. She decided to find and interview cancer patients who had experienced what she calls 'radical remission' from their cancer.

She also decided to travel the globe and interview fifty non-Western, alternative healers about their approaches to cancer. Since her initial dissertation research, she has continued to conduct hundreds of interviews and analyzed over a thousand written cases of radical remission. What she found was "more than seventy-five different factors that may hypothetically play a role in radical remission, but when she tabulated the frequency of each factor, she found that nine of those seventy-five factors kept coming up again and again in almost every interview. "The nine key factors for Radical Remission are:

- Radically changing your diet

- Taking control of your health

- Following your intuition

- Using herbs and supplements

- Releasing suppressed emotions

- Increasing positive emotions

- Embracing social support

- Deepening your spiritual connection

- Having strong reasons for living"

Dr. Turner, like Dr. Rankin, is quick to admit that she is not opposed to conventional cancer treatment, including surgery, chemotherapy and radiation and goes on to say that many cancer survivors owe their freedom from the disease to these traditional treatments. There are also many who have done a combination of traditional treatments and alternative treatments. And there are those who have been able to achieve their radical remission by using only alternative type treatments or therapies. Throughout her book, she shares some of the personal stories of these survivors and they are truly well worth the read!

In the conclusion of Dr. Turner's book, she starts with the following quote, "He who has health, has hope. And he who has hope, has everything," from Philosopher, Thomas Carlyle. I don't believe there could be a more important point for any patient facing a frightening diagnosis – whether it is cancer or some other chronic disease – that we have hope! As she states, cancer can be caused by toxins, viruses, bacteria, genetic mutation or cellular breakdown and what appears to play a pivotal role is the state of our *body-mind-spirit* system; how our bodies are able to deal with these potential threats to our well-being. Add to this mix the "wonderful, complex reality of individuality..." she says and that radical remission survivors "constantly remind me that no two people on this planet are the same and therefore no two prescriptions for health will be the same."

Dr. Turner's singular goal in writing her book is also the same reason that I am writing mine and that is *empowerment*!

When we first get the diagnosis of cancer, it is truly paralyzing – the fear of the treatments, the fear of death, recognizing our own mortality….it is a wonder that any of us can get out of bed and face another day, let alone be able to rally and face that new day with hope, joy, optimism, gratitude and love. Wouldn't it be different if all our health practitioners were schooled on the importance of hope, optimism and the unique journey of each individual? Can you imagine how different it might be for us when we walked out of our doctor's office after being told that our body is demonstrating some cell mutation and now we need to discover what might be causing the mutation and explore the avenues for treating it? That sounds so much better to me than "you have cancer; it's already spread; we're setting you up for surgery next week, followed by chemotherapy and then some radiation. Without treatment, you probably only have a couple of years left." Geez! I feel the panic just writing that stuff! It is so refreshing to read *Radical Remission* and to learn of the many people who have healed, against insurmountable odds! Every cancer patient should be flooded with these kinds of stories to give them hope!

As mentioned earlier in this chapter, sometimes you appear to be doing everything right – eating a great diet full of nutrient dense foods, you exercise, meditate and still your disease continues to manifest itself. What else can you possibly do? Well, maybe now's the time to go on a Journey – and that's exactly what I did next!

CHAPTER 12

THE JOURNEY

Recently, I was invited to be on a local radio program, along with another cancer "thriver" to speak of our journeys and the types of treatment we have chosen. My co-presenter was a beautiful young woman who was diagnosed with breast cancer in her late thirties. Initially, she did undergo a lumpectomy but she refused any further traditional care such as chemo or radiation, and instead had the means to be able to go to Switzerland and attend the Paracelsus Clinic. (Remember Dr. Rau and the *Swiss Secret to Optimal Health*? That's his clinic.) She is very nearly five years out from her initial diagnosis and is doing very well.

She has come to love her cancer and all the enlightenment and growth it has brought her. She has even done a fabulous painting of the tumor as seen on ultrasound. She pointed out that her tumor looked like a fetus in the mother's womb. Through counseling, she realized that perhaps it was her terrible sorrow of not being able to have children that brought on her cancer. When she returned to her home in Antigua, she became a staunch advocate for organic farming and pure drinking water. She set up a studio where she has a lending library, has regular meditation sessions and yoga classes.

It was a really powerful feeling to be speaking the same healing language together on the radio – expressing our mutual sentiments that cancer gives us a wonderful opportunity to learn, to grow, to improve the quality of our lives. After the interview, she looked at me and said, "You have more work to do." My eyes started to tear up immediately, as I was still trying to "get my power" back as my latest tumor marker results were up and the latest CT scan showed a tumor that had grown thirteen centimeters in five months. Surgery was being recommended again.

She went on to tell me about another aspect of her personal treatment plan – which was initially counseling but then she was referred to a book called *The Journey* by Brandon Bays and was encouraged to take 'the Journey'. She explained a bit about how one goes about this 'journey' and offered to loan me the book.

A few weeks later, I took her up on the offer and borrowed her book. The cover states that the book is "A practical Guide to Healing Your Life and Setting Yourself Free". Okay, let's go! The book caught my attention right away and before I was halfway through, I had already done some initial 'Journey work' on myself and came up with some astounding results! Brandon Bays has you 'peel the layers of the onion of your life' - so to speak, by feeling or experiencing an emotion and then trying to get under or behind that emotion to see what provoked it.

As an example, for my first attempt at this process, I was on my way to my first yoga class and I was nervous and wishing I hadn't promised my friend that I would come. I knew in my head I wanted to make yoga a regular practice in my life so why was I having these feelings? Okay, so the first layer was nervousness. I was feeling nervous about attending. Now, peeling away that layer – what was under or behind that nervous feeling? It was self-consciousness. Hmmm – okay – but why? Granted, I don't have the best figure in the world but it isn't *that* bad! What was under that self-consciousness? It was fear! But why fear? Was there anything else under that layer of fear? Not that I could sense, so what was I afraid of?

A few more minutes of thought and a light bulb went on! I grew up as a military dependent. My Dad got re-assigned every three or four years so that meant another move, starting off in a new place, with no friends, not knowing my way around the new school, etc. I never was able to sleep and would literally get sick the night before my first day at a new school or a new school year. I had a hard time making friends and it seemed like weeks of loneliness and isolation each time we moved. So now I felt enlightened – that's where this fear was coming from – but I was not that child anymore. I was a self-confident adult, able to meet and greet people and to easily make friends. Pleased with myself for unraveling my anxieties, I went on to enjoy my first yoga class and have been happily attending ever since!

A few nights later and after a few more chapters in Brandon Bays' book, I decided to do another 'onion peeling' session. I successfully peeled back the layers of my emotions and what came to light was quite profound and surprising to me, but made so much sense!   I was discovering and unburdening my soul with some pretty heavy baggage but now felt that I really needed to do 'The Journey' with an experienced guide, someone who would be able to help me when I got stuck and was unable to go any further.

A few days later, I was at my monthly chiropractic appointment and as I feel such a kindred spirit in my practitioner, I took this latest book to show her. To my surprise, Dr. Taylor said she loved that book and offered to assist me with 'The Journey' as she had done this before. Wow! What a surprise and another wonderful coincidence! Ask for something and it is placed right in front of you!   I had some hesitation about doing this 'Journey' with someone I knew so well. I really didn't feel comfortable possibly revealing some deep, dark secrets of my past, but on the other hand, when might an experienced practitioner show up on this island? We set up a time and meeting place for Good Friday, a local holiday here in Antigua. That night, as I read a couple more chapters, I learned that when doing 'The Journey,' it is important to *NOT* tell the story but rather just the emotions associated with your particular story. So, my fears about having to relay embarrassing details of my life were allayed and on Good Friday....we did the 'Journey'!

Brandon Bays spells out the whole process for you, step-by-step, even providing the dialogue. There are actually two 'Journeys' you do with this process – the first is called the Emotional Journey which was similar to what I had been experimenting with myself, peeling back the layers of emotion and analyzing what was behind them. It was a good thing that there was a box of tissues nearby, as this particular Journey really was emotional. Long past episodes of emotionally traumatic events came to light and were dealt with. You have a mentor of your choosing along with you on both these Journeys and although he or she is not physically present with you, their guidance, support and assurances are felt as if they were. There is a point in this Journey where understanding and forgiveness is sought and eventually expressed. You come back up, layer by layer, releasing the emotions along the way, and when this Journey was complete, I felt such a strong sense of inner peace, inner stillness, and quiet. At this point, you are given some time to be alone and absorb all that you have just gone through.

The second Journey is what Brandon Bays calls the Physical Journey, where you imagine yourself taking a trip into your body, allowing your mind to dictate what specific area it decides to guide you to. Again, you have your mentor along with you on this Journey. When you eventually arrive at your destination, you are asked to describe what you see.

For me it was my tumor – I saw it as a somewhat hollowed cavern or cave and my mentor and I were inside it. The walls were vascular – blood vessels large and small, running all through it, creating a type of lighting that I can still see in my mind but can't find the words to describe. Like the Emotional Journey, there is a point in this one where you confront a person who has been the source – in my case – of shame, humiliation and powerlessness. And similar to the previous Journey, you come to a place of understanding and forgiveness. At this point, you are asked to return to the place in your body that you were guided to initially and once again, to describe it – especially noting any changes that might have occurred. This time, as I stepped inside this hollowed tumor, the word that immediately came to mind was 'death star'. The change was so dramatic! There was nothing living, it was all gray and dark, with no sign of all that red vasculature that was lining all the walls on the first visit.

The two Journeys took about two hours in total and at the conclusion, I truly felt drained, empty, but free, light and happy! On my drive home, I started to giggle when I realized I was craving a cigarette (I hadn't smoked in over 30 years!). I was also craving some rich, dark chocolate and, if not a cigarette, then at least a good cup of coffee!

It's been several months since I did those Journeys and I am happy to report that I still feel that same feeling of being free, happy and released!

I might add here that, subsequently, I have gone back for another CT scan and the tumor, although still present, did not grow a single millimeter and the radiologist proclaimed it as a "stable disease". Meanwhile, the tumor markers took a dramatic down turn – perhaps reflecting that my tumor truly is a death star!

CHAPTER 13

YOU'VE COME A LONG WAY BABY OR LOOK WHO'S BACK!

It's been fifteen years since I was first diagnosed with this disease. There have been a lot of ups and downs and since I still have to get those tumor marker blood draws, there is always the potential for that initial shock if the markers have made a dramatic jump...in the wrong direction. It used to hit me pretty hard and my way of dealing with it was to call my husband, call my sisters, call my kids, tell my boss....but one time when this happened, I got a whole new perspective!

I had held it together until I got to my chiropractic appointment with my dear friend, Dr. Janet Taylor, then it all came pouring out...along with quite a few tears! Janet calmly told me about Byron Katie and a process she developed called "The Work". You express what your stressful thought is and of course mine was, "My tumor is back!" The next question is, "Is it true?" And, of course, I answered "Yes!" The next question is "Can you absolutely know that it's true?" And when I reflected on that, I realized the answer would be, "No, I just knew that the blood test markers were elevated"....but maybe, I speculated, just maybe, they were elevated for some other reason.

The next question is "How do you react when you believe that thought?

And, of course, if I think my disease is back, I am upset; I feel like a failure; I'm afraid! The next question is "Who would you be without that thought?" Well, of course, I would be happy, overjoyed, and radiant! For me, we didn't even really need to finish the exercise because at that moment a BIG light bulb popped up! I can *choose* how I want to react – I can continue with my "Woe is Me" diatribe or I can stand up straight and be strong, confident, and positive.

That night I decided to read up on Byron Katie. I ordered a couple of books and read some online articles. Something I read that night really became a pivotal point for me and I like to use it in my counseling of others. I'm not sure whether or not this is from Byron Katie, but it was something I came across doing my research that evening, and it really resonated with me. The story was about a woman with breast cancer. She was asked to write down the story of her life on one piece of paper. When finished, she handed it over to the counselor and after reading it, the paper was handed back to her. She was told that she had written the story of her life as a *victim*. Now, she was told to turn the paper over and re-write the story of her life – but this time, write the story as the *heroine*. Wow!

I'm beginning to realize that this Healing Journey is not one with an endpoint, a final destination – that is, unless we count the day that we finally graduate and get to advance to the next world.

But as long as we are on this earthly plane, we have the guarantee that there will be obstacles and we have the choice to have those obstacles be stumbling blocks or instead, another opportunity for learning and growth. My daughter-in-law pointed out to me that if my disease never came back after my first obstacle and learning – the *Eat to Live* book and diet – I would be a totally different person than who I am today.

Another poignant moment for me was when several years ago, my son said to me, when I was tearfully sharing with him that my markers had gone back up, "Mom, if it took this disease to make you grow into the person you've become, just think what the future holds." So, in the words of a very wise person, I can choose to be the victim or I can choose to be the heroine. I choose to be Starry Jones! But this Starry Jones has a new mission in life. I have rekindled that joy of living life to the fullest, but have given up the imagined life of the child movie star and instead, taken on the role of a happy, healthy, (maybe even spunky), wellness advocate.

Epilogue

As I sit here trying to find the right words for ending my book, I take the road of the procrastinator and switch to Facebook. But there, the second story down, was a post from one of my Integrative Nutrition classmates asking for prayers and donations for her daughter's good friend, a sixteen year old girl who has just been diagnosed with ovarian cancer! What a tragic impetus that is, to finish this book and pray that in some way it will help others along their journey. This has been my goal from the beginning of this book, to be able to share my learning and to hope in some way, I can help others along this path. I warmly invite you to contact me and allow me the privilege of walking alongside you on your healing journey.

∞

"At whatever time highly-skilled physicians shall have developed the healing of illnesses by means of foods, and shall make provision for simple foods, and shall prohibit humankind from living as slaves to their lustful appetites, it is certain that the incidence of chronic and diversified illnesses will abate, and the general health of all mankind will be much improved. This is destined to come about."

'Abdu'l-Baha', from the Baha'i Writings

Resources

Chapter 2

Eat to Live by Joel Fuhrman, M.D.

Chapter 5

The Swiss Secret to Optimal Health by Thomas Rau, M.D. with Susan Wyler

Killing Cancer – Not People by Robert G. Wright

Budwig Protocol – www.budwigcenter.com

Crazy, Sexy Cancer Tips, by Kris Carr; www.kriscarr.com

Ann Wigmore Natural Health Institute – www.annwigmore.org

Fat, Sick and Nearly Dead, a Joe Cross Film; www.rebootwithjoe.com; www.fatsickandnearlydead.com

Chapter 8

www.findmyfamily.org

Chapter 9

Proof of Heaven by Eben Alexander, M.D.; www.lifebeyonddeath.net

Dying to be Me by Anita Moorjani;
www.anitamoorjani.com

Chapter 10

Institute of Integrative Nutrition –
www.integrativenutrition.com

Chapter 11

Mind over Medicine by Lissa Rankin, M.D.

Radical Remission by Kelly A. Turner, Ph.D.

Chapter 12

The Journey by Brandon Bays

Chapter 13

The Work of Byron Katie – www.thework.com

Other Resources used but not specifically mentioned in this book:

The Tapping Solution by Nick Ortner – using EFT – Emotional Freedom Technique

Clean by Alejandro Junger, M.D.

My Beautiful Life, How I conquered Cancer Naturally by Mina Dobic

Videos

Fat Sick and Nearly Dead Joe Cross

You Can Heal Your Life by Louise Hay and Friends

Forks over Knives

*The Cure Is***   I *Loved* this one

****